Report Number: C43-022R-2003

Guide to Sun Microsystems Java Plug-in Security

I0411027

Network Applications Team
Of the
Systems and Network Attack Center (SNAC)

Dated: 8 December 2003
Version 1.0

National Security Agency
9800 Savage Rd. Suite 6704
Ft. Meade, MD 20755-6704

- **Do not attempt to implement any of the settings in this guide without first testing in a non-operational environment.**

- This document is only a guide containing recommended security settings. It is not meant to replace well-structured policy or sound judgment. Furthermore this guide does not address site-specific configuration issues. Care must be taken when implementing this guide to address local operational and policy concerns.

- The security changes described in this document only apply to Microsoft Windows 2000 systems and should not be applied to any other Windows versions or operating systems.

- This document may contain recommended settings for the system Registry. Java can be severely impaired or disabled with incorrect changes or accidental deletions when using a Registry editor (Regedt32.exe or Regedit.exe) to change the system configuration.

- Currently, there is no **undo** command for deletions within the Registry. Registry editor prompts the user to confirm the deletions if **Confirm on Delete** (Regedt32.exe) is selected from the options menu. When a key is deleted, the message does not include the name of the key being deleted. Therefore, check selection carefully before proceeding.

- SOFTWARE IS PROVIDED "AS IS" AND ANY EXPRESS OR IMPLIED WARRANTIES, INCLUDING, BUT NOT LIMITED TO, THE IMPLIED WARRANTIES OF MERCHANTABILITY AND FITNESS FOR A PARTICULAR PURPOSE ARE EXPRESSLY DISCLAIMED. IN NO EVENT SHALL THE CONTRIBUTORS BE LIABLE FOR ANY DIRECT, INDIRECT, INCIDENTAL, SPECIAL, EXEMPLARY, OR CONSEQUENTIAL DAMAGES (INCLUDING, BUT NOT LIMITED TO, PROCUREMENT OF SUBSTITUTE GOODS OR SERVICES; LOSS OF USE, DATA, OR PROFITS; OR BUSINESS INTERRUPTION) HOWEVER CAUSED AND ON ANY THEORY OF LIABILITY, WHETHER IN CONTRACT, STRICT LIABILITY, OR TORT (INCLUDING NEGLIGENCE OR OTHERWISE) ARISING IN ANY WAY OUT OF THE USE OF THIS SOFTWARE, EVEN IF ADVISED OF THE POSSIBILITY OF SUCH DAMAGE.

- See Microsoft's web page for the latest changes or modifications to the Windows 2000 operating system and Sun's web page for Java.

Acknowledgements

This document is highly dependent upon an original document written by Curt Doernberg.

Trademark Information

Java is a registered trademark of Sun Microsystems Corporation.

Microsoft, Windows 2000, Internet Explorer are either registered trademarks or trademarks of Microsoft Corporation in the U.S.A. and other countries.

All other names are registered trademarks or trademarks of their respective companies.

Introduction

Web browsers are fundamentally designed to deliver web pages from a web server. However, through plug-in technology, most web browsers can be enabled to deliver additional features such as Java programs, known as applets. The need for trusted applets has increased with applet popularity; however, signed applets within a web browser can be a greater risk than unsigned applets. This document focuses on the Sun Microsystems 1.4.2 Java Runtime Environment (JRE) Java Plug-in available with Netscape 7.1 and for Internet Explorer 6.0 on a Microsoft Windows Platform.

This document is developed to provide guidance to an Information Technology Administrator. It is vital to client and network security to understand the risks involved with applets in web browsers. The document is not necessarily a how-to guide, but more an information guide to the existence and usage of settings. There are already numerous how-to guides, some of which are listed in the References section.

Many current online resources provide outdated information with respect to the ever-changing versions within web browsers. Even though some of the web browser relevant information is not accurate, most of the JRE security model has not changed since the large overhaul that created the Java 2 security model. However, there have been some important certificate specific changes since the initial release of the J2SE, which will be detailed further in this document. The current Java version has been out for a few years; the next major release, Java, 1.5, is expected to be in Spring 2004.

Java Applets

As mentioned briefly above, an applet is merely a program written in the Java programming language with the intent to run in a web browser environment. Applets can also be written for a local file system. The standard permissions between the two default scenarios differ greatly. As a general rule, the web browser applet has more restrictive security permissions than does an applet within the local file system.

Ironically, from a security perspective, a signed applet is a greater risk than an unsigned applet. From within the web browser, an applet is either unsigned or signed. The unsigned applets can only run within the very restrictive standard applet security model. The signed applets will run with AllPermission privileges, provided that the security conscious user chooses "Accept" in response to the generic warning dialog. It is through this feeble mechanism that signed applets are more harmful than unsigned ones. Keep in mind that even an attacker can sign his/her applet in hope that the end-user will accept the dialog window. Fortunately, there is still hope for trusting and securing signed applets. The Java 2 security model provides extremely fine-grained security controls on all Java permissions through the use of a Policy file. Further details are given later in this document.

JRE Plug-in

The Java 2 Platform, Standard Edition, J2SE, has two different releases, the JRE and SDK. The JRE, geared more toward the end-user, provides the libraries, Java virtual machine, and other components necessary for the user to run applets and applications written in the Java programming language. It does not contain tools and utilities, such as compilers or debuggers for developing applets and applications. Such tools are available with the SDK, which is a superset that includes the JRE.

The JRE is responsible for the security of Java Applets, including behavior that is appropriate to policy, as well as verifying digital signatures. The Java 2 security model is intended to grant privileges to signed code based on URL of origin and properties of the signature. Unfortunately, the default web browser configuration has a much simpler model: an applet with a signature that the user trusts gets the privilege java.security.AllPermission – the full functionality of the Java programming language. In order to administratively prevent the user from allowing applications with untrusted signatures from running with full permissions, the following actions must be performed:

- The java.policy file must be modified to change the default prompt behavior to actually enforce the abiding policy.

- If granting any applets extra privileges, the following steps must be performed:
    - The cacerts CA store must be modified to include only those CAs who should be allowed to vouch for the right to use possibly dangerous Java permissions.
    - If giving permissions based on specific code-signing certificates, a pubcerts keystore must be created to include these certificates.
    - The java.policy file should be modified to add privileges for each applet executing with extra privileges.

- Finally, the key store(s) and java.policy file must be replicated to all computers requiring applet access.

These required actions are described in greater detail throughout the rest of this document.

Administrative and Developer tools

The Java Runtime Environment now includes an administrative GUI, the Java Plug-in Control Panel, and a simple debugging applet, the Java Console. These tools can be found in the Windows Control Panel folder.

• Java Plug-in Control Panel

The Java Plug-in Control Panel allows a user to modify the default Java plug-in settings. The control panel not only allows a user to specify the JRE version, but also permits advanced browser, cache and proxy settings. The most noteworthy feature of the control panel is the addition of the Certificate panel. As of Java 1.4.x, Sun Microsystems no longer uses the browser certificate store for certificate storage. In Java 1.4.x and later, a signed applet must use the Java Control Panel certificate panel for certificate storage. This feature has created controversy and many wrongly configured certificate settings. Lastly, a new feature of the Control Panel is the automatic Java Update panel. This feature will allow various levels of automatic updates for Java to occur from Sun.

• Console

The Java Console is a JRE feature that allows for basic Java program debugging. The Console features options that allow standard debugging operations such as: memory usage analysis, garbage collection, display cached objects, and various informative printouts during run-time.

Web Browsers

Internet Explorer (IE) features the Microsoft Java Virtual Machine (MSJVM) for running applets within IE, version 6 and prior. The MSJVM, based upon Java 1.1, is more than 5 years old. However, Microsoft has announced that the new Java .NET architecture will replace the existing MSJVM within IE. Microsoft will continue to support the MSJVM until September 2004. Currently, Microsoft is offering migration guidance, http://www.microsoft.com/mscorp/java/, in transitioning applets written for MSJVM to a new .NET framework or third party JRE solution. See the Sun Microsystems webpage on migrating from MSJVM to JRE solution, http://java.sun.com/j2se/1.4.2/docs/guide/deployment/deployment-guide/upgrade-guide/.

The MSJVM will install by default with IE, unlike the additional setup required to install the Sun Microsystems J2SE 1.4.x. Internet Explorer will run correctly with both the MSJVM and JRE plug-in installed. However, only one Java framework can be the default. It is recommended that the JRE be selected as the default application for Java Applets. Usually IE is installed prior to the JRE installation. During the plug-in installation, a prompt, see Figure 1, will allow the user to enable JRE Java Plug-in as the default VM for each browser installed.

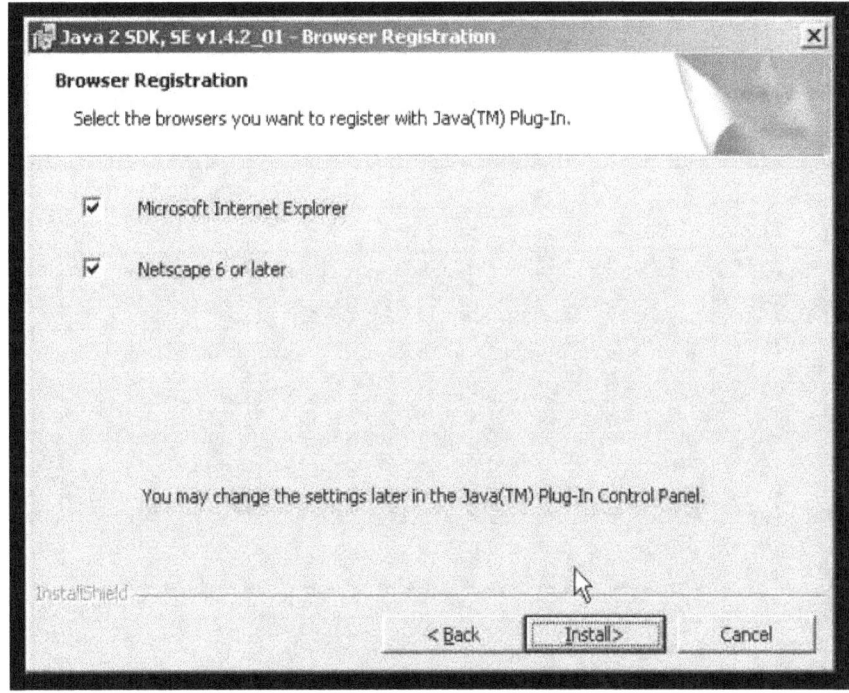

Figure 1 JRE Installation Selection

Netscape 7.1 includes the J2SE 1.4.x JRE from Sun Microsystems. There is no need for an additional java plug-in installation. Additional information about the JRE keystore is detailed later on in this document.

Applet Development Lifecycle

The applet development lifecycle involves not only the usual developer and administrative tasks but also both the applet signer and receiver processes. This document will primarily focus on the receiver process phase during applet development.

Signer Process

The signer process as the code signer of applets involves numerous steps. First, the keys needed to sign the applet have to be created through the key generation step. Next, the JAR file needs to be signed. Finally, the public key certificate needs to be exported, along with a list of required permissions. Each of these steps are outside the scope of this document and is described in detail within the Sun Microsystems website,
http://java.sun.com/docs/books/tutorial/security1.2/toolsign/signer.html.

Receiver Process

The receiver process of receiving signed applets involves two main steps: importing the certificates and constructing the policy file. As an initial process, there needs to occur additional steps, such as creating a keystore for public certificates and understanding both the permissions and policy files.

• Java's Certificate Authority Store - cacerts

The certificate store used by the Java plug-in is different than the one used by Netscape or IE for storage of user certificates. The default location is C:\Program Files\Java\j2re1.4.0\lib\security\cacerts. This difference in location has created many difficulties for both the developers and users of applets. For example, there is little documentation alerting users of this change in procedure from Java 1.3 to 1.4. Furthermore, there is no synchronization between the browser certificate store and the Java plug-in store. Future implementations of Java and Netscape may include certificate verification and may allow for better integration of these two certificate stores.

• Tools

Sun Microsystems has developed some tools to aid a developer in secure applet development. The tools are freely available for Solaris, Linux and Windows platforms at http://java.sun.com/j2se/1.4.2/docs/tooldocs/tools.html

Appletviewer

The appletviewer, a GUI applet, allows a developer to run an applet outside the usual web browser environment.

Policytool

The policytool is a GUI-based applet that aides in the creation of a Java policy file. The policytool not only provides correct syntax, but also reduces complexities inherent within a policy file.

Keytool

The Sun Microsystems documentation describes the keytool in the following manner:

> "keytool is a key and certificate management utility. It enables users to administer their own public/private key pairs and associated certificates for use in self-authentication or data integrity and authentication services, using digital signatures. It also allows users to cache the public keys (in the form of certificates) of their communicating peers.
>
> A certificate is a digitally signed statement from one entity (person, company, etc.), saying that the public key (and some other information) of some other entity has a particular value. When data is digitally signed, the signature can be verified to check the data integrity and authenticity. Integrity means that the data has not been modified or tampered with, and authenticity means the data indeed comes from whoever claims to have created and signed it. "

keytool stores the keys and certificates in a so-called keystore. The default keystore implementation implements the keystore as a file. It protects private keys with a password.

Jarsigner

The jarsigner tool is used to primarily sign JAR files and also to verify the signatures and integrity of signed JAR files. A Java Archive (JAR) file is a specialized zip archive, such that a JAR file packages many Java class files for ease of distribution and compression.

- **Adding or Importing Keys**

The key importation process utilizes the keytool along with the JRE keystore. This paper includes brief demonstrations of how to view, add, and remove keys from the default keystore.

As illustrated in Figure 2, list all CAs used by Java by setting the path to include the Java bin directory, changing into the directory containing the cacerts, and running the following command:

keytool –list –keystore cacerts

More detailed reports can be generated by adding the –v option to the previous command.

```
C:\WINNT\System32\cmd.exe                                               _|□|X

Microsoft Windows 2000 [Version 5.00.2195]
(C) Copyright 1985-1999 Microsoft Corp.

C:\>set Path=%Path%;C:\Program Files\Java\j2re1.4.0_03\bin

C:\>cd "C:\Program Files\Java\j2re1.4.0_03\lib\security"

C:\Program Files\Java\j2re1.4.0_03\lib\security>keytool -list -keystore cacerts
Enter keystore password:  changeit

Keystore type: jks
Keystore provider: SUN

Your keystore contains 10 entries

thawtepersonalfreemailca, Feb 12, 1999, trustedCertEntry,
Certificate fingerprint (MD5): 1E:74:C3:86:3C:0C:35:C5:3E:C2:7F:EF:3C:AA:3C:D9
thawtepersonalbasicca, Feb 12, 1999, trustedCertEntry,
Certificate fingerprint (MD5): E6:0B:D2:C9:CA:2D:88:DB:1A:71:0E:4B:78:EB:02:41
verisignclass3ca, Jun 29, 1998, trustedCertEntry,
Certificate fingerprint (MD5): 78:2A:02:DF:DB:2E:14:D5:A7:5F:0A:DF:B6:8E:9C:5D
thawtepersonalpremiumca, Feb 12, 1999, trustedCertEntry,
Certificate fingerprint (MD5): 3A:B2:DE:22:9A:20:93:49:F9:ED:C8:D2:8A:E7:68:0D
thawteserverca, Feb 12, 1999, trustedCertEntry,
Certificate fingerprint (MD5): C5:70:C4:A2:ED:53:78:0C:C8:10:53:81:64:CB:D0:1D
verisignclass4ca, Jun 29, 1998, trustedCertEntry,
Certificate fingerprint (MD5): 1B:D1:AD:17:8B:7F:22:13:24:F5:26:E2:5D:4E:B9:10
verisignserverca, Jun 29, 1998, trustedCertEntry,
Certificate fingerprint (MD5): 74:7B:82:03:43:F0:00:9E:6B:B3:EC:47:BF:85:A5:93
verisignclass1ca, Jun 29, 1998, trustedCertEntry,
Certificate fingerprint (MD5): 51:86:E8:1F:BC:B1:C3:71:B5:18:10:DB:5F:DC:F6:20
thawtepremiumserverca, Feb 12, 1999, trustedCertEntry,
Certificate fingerprint (MD5): 06:9F:69:79:16:66:90:02:1B:8C:8C:A2:C3:07:6F:3A
verisignclass2ca, Jun 29, 1998, trustedCertEntry,
Certificate fingerprint (MD5): EC:40:7D:2B:76:52:67:05:2C:EA:F2:3A:4F:65:F0:D8

C:\Program Files\Java\j2re1.4.0_03\lib\security>
```

Figure 2 - Listing Certificates

Your local security policy should determine which certificates should remain in the trusted CAs store. In order to implement this policy, examples of adding and removing a certificate are provided below. The following two examples are for illustration only and are not recommended for implementation exactly as shown. Both of these examples assume that the PATH has been set to include the Java bin directory.

As illustrated in Figure 3, running the following command will delete the CA specified by <Alias name>.

```
keytool -delete -alias <Alias name> -keystore cacerts
```

This is how to remove any CAs that are installed by default but are not trusted by your policy.

```
C:\WINNT\System32\cmd.exe                                               _|□|X

C:\Program Files\Java\j2re1.4.0_03\lib\security>keytool -delete -alias verisignc
lass4ca -keystore cacerts
Enter keystore password:  changeit

C:\Program Files\Java\j2re1.4.0_03\lib\security>_
```

Figure 3 - Deleting A CA Certificate

As illustrated in Figure 4, by running the following command, a new CA whose file is specified by <CertFileName> is imported into the CA's store.

```
keytool -import -trustcacerts -alias <Alias Name> -file <CertFileName>
```

Notice that keytool requires you to read the certificate information and fingerprints and type 'yes' in order to accept the certificate.

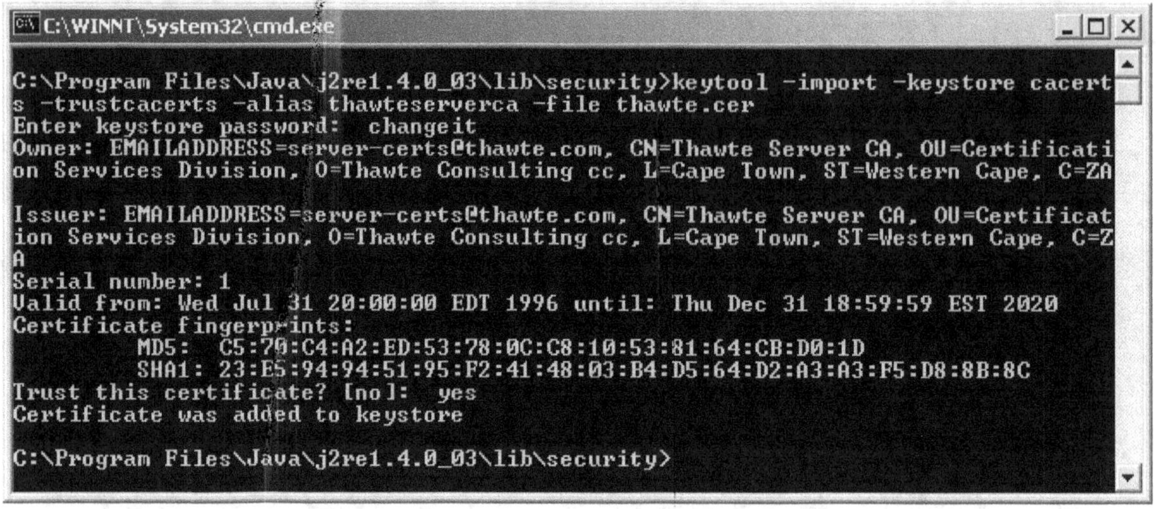

Figure 4 - Importing A CA Certificate

The end result of these operations is that the cacerts file will contain those certificates that match your organization's policy.

- **Creating the pubcerts keystore**

In order to grant permissions to any code signed by a particular code-signing certificate, Java must first have this certificate on file in a keystore. This document will assume that this keystore is called pubcerts and located in the same directory as cacerts. To place code-signing certificates in the keystore, perform the following steps for each certificate to be imported:

- Set the path and change into the directory containing cacerts as shown in Figure 2.

- Copy the certificate into the C:\Program Files\Java\j2re1.4.0\lib\security directory.

- Run the following command:

```
keytool -import -alias <cert alias> -file <cert filename> -keystore pubcerts
```

- Enter the keystore password.

- Validate that this is the correct certificate. Type 'yes' in response to the question "Trust this certificate?" if this is the correct certificate.

This will import the file named by <cert filename> into the keystore pubcerts where it will be known as <cert alias>. In the example shown in Figure 5, the certificate in the file curt.cer is imported with the alias Curt.

```
C:\Program Files\Java\j2re1.4.0_03\lib\security>dir /w
 Volume in drive C has no label.
 Volume Serial Number is F004-F2A9

 Directory of C:\Program Files\Java\j2re1.4.0_03\lib\security

[.]                      [..]                      cacerts
curt.cer                 java.policy               java.security
local_policy.jar         US_export_policy.jar
               6 File(s)         24,102 bytes
               2 Dir(s)    2,400,264,192 bytes free

C:\Program Files\Java\j2re1.4.0_03\lib\security>keytool -import -alias Curt -fil
e curt.cer -keystore pubcerts
Enter keystore password:  changeit
Owner: CN=Curt Doernberg, OU=Jabuti Lab, O=C43, L=Linthicum, ST=MD, C=US
Issuer: CN=PowerEdge Netscape CA, OU=Applications and Architecture Division, O=S
ystem and Network Attack Center, L=Linthicum, ST=MD, C=US
Serial number: a
Valid from: Thu Mar 20 10:12:24 EST 2003 until: Fri Mar 19 10:12:24 EST 2004
Certificate fingerprints:
         MD5:  2C:DF:8C:80:50:8E:09:D4:4B:72:BB:E6:11:1E:D3:8D
         SHA1: 25:21:CB:AB:1D:07:12:70:96:F8:54:8F:8F:C1:14:63:02:C1:F6:25
Trust this certificate? [no]:  yes
Certificate was added to keystore

C:\Program Files\Java\j2re1.4.0_03\lib\security>dir /w
 Volume in drive C has no label.
 Volume Serial Number is F004-F2A9

 Directory of C:\Program Files\Java\j2re1.4.0_03\lib\security

[.]                      [..]                      cacerts
curt.cer                 java.policy               java.security
local_policy.jar         pubcerts                  US_export_policy.jar
               7 File(s)         25,337 bytes
               2 Dir(s)    2,400,260,096 bytes free

C:\Program Files\Java\j2re1.4.0_03\lib\security>_
```

Figure 5 - Importing A Publisher Certificate

- **Setting the keystore**

Before the Policy Tool can link permissions to the keys in the pubcerts keystore, it must first have the keystore location in the policy file. To generate this entry, perform the following steps:

- Open the java.policy file with the Policy Tool.

- In the Edit menu, select Change Keystore. This will cause the window in Figure 6 to appear.

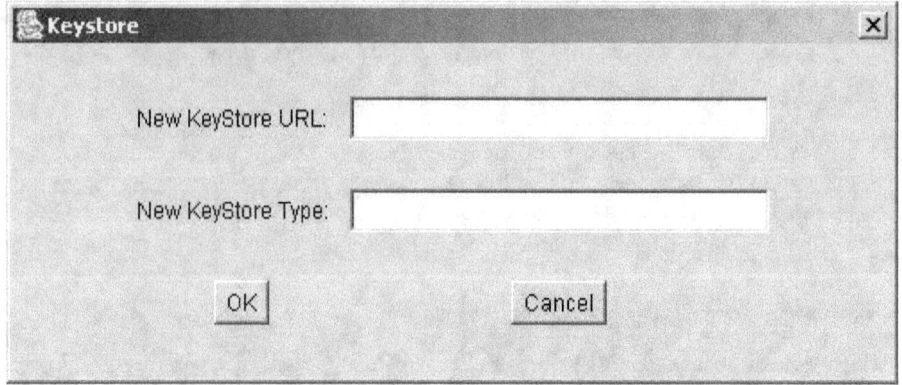

Figure 6 - Keystore Modification

- Next to New KeyStore URL, type the following:

```
file:/C:/Program Files/Java/j2re1.4.0_03/lib/security/pubcerts
```

- Next to New Keystore Type, type the following:

```
JKS
```

- Click OK. The policy tool should now have a keystore entry like Figure 7.

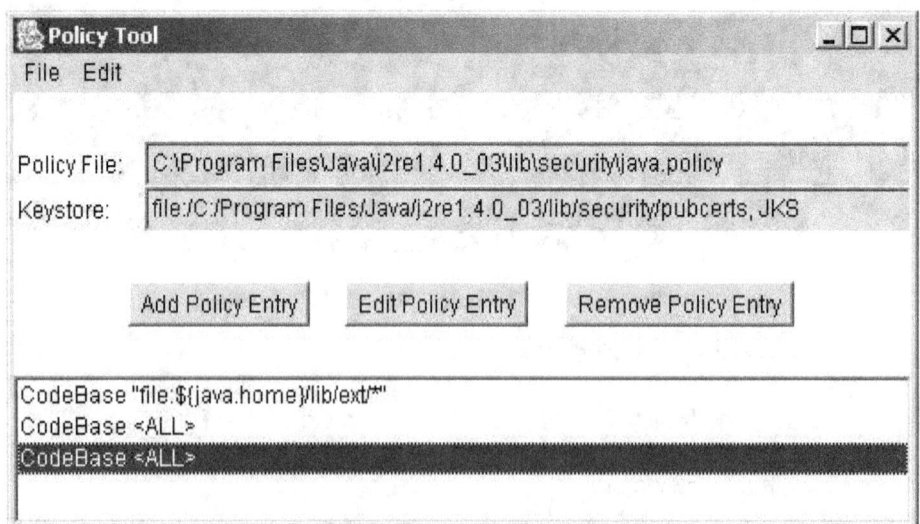

Figure 7 - Policy Tool with Keystore Entry

- Save the Policy File.

- **Permissions in the Java 2 JRE**

The Java 2 security model includes the ability to specifically grant 18 groups of some 80 permissions to applets. These 80 plus permissions include such privileges

UNCLASSIFIED

12

as: createClassLoader, read/write/execute file, connect/listen socket, accessClipboard or any such action that represents access to a system resource. A particularly descriptive document detailing the purpose and risk of each Java permission has been written by Sun Microsystems, http://java.sun.com/j2se/1.4.2/docs/guide/security/permissions.html.

- **Policy File**

The java.security.policy object represents the Policy file, a configuration file for the applet permissions. The system wide policy file, java.policy, is the default file; while, the user specific policy, .java.policy, is optional. There is a third built-in policy file, java.security that is only used when both the default and optional policy files cannot be located. These policy files use a grant entry that uses the following format: an optional signedBy, an optional codeBase, an optional principal and permission entries. The signedBy entry is an alias for a certificate stored within the keystore. The codeBase, a URL, can be either a file location or a true HTTP address. The principal entry, class and name pair, is mainly used as a keystore alias. An applet will need explicit permission for a particular action. An exception is that the applet will have read permission of files and subdirectories from the same URL or location of the applet's location. Additional explanations can be discovered on Sun's web site, http://java.sun.com/j2se/1.4.2/docs/guide/security/PolicyFiles.html

- **Add usePolicy Permission**

The signed applets have to be forced to adhere to the policy, by the Java plug-in granting the "usePolicy" privilege to all applets. If this step is not completed, only the less restrictive default policy file will be enforced for the applets. To ensure the correct policy file is used, one needs to accomplish the following steps:

- Open the Policytool application c:\Program Files\Java\j2re.1.4.0_03\bin\policytool.exe. (The policy tool may give an error message about inability to find a different policy file, just ignore the message.)
- In the File menu, select Open.
- Select the file c:\Program Files\Java\j2re.1.4.0_03\lib\security\java.policy. The application window should now look like Figure 8.

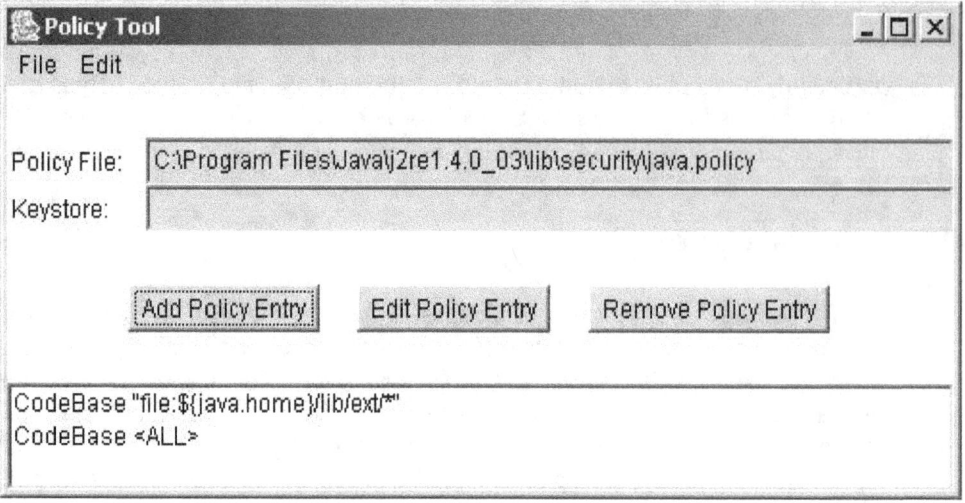

Figure 8 - java.policy initial settings

- Click Add Policy Entry.
- Click Add Permission.
- Pull down Permission: to select RuntimePermission.
- Pull down Target Name: to select usePolicy.
- Click OK. The permission to be added should now look like Figure 9.

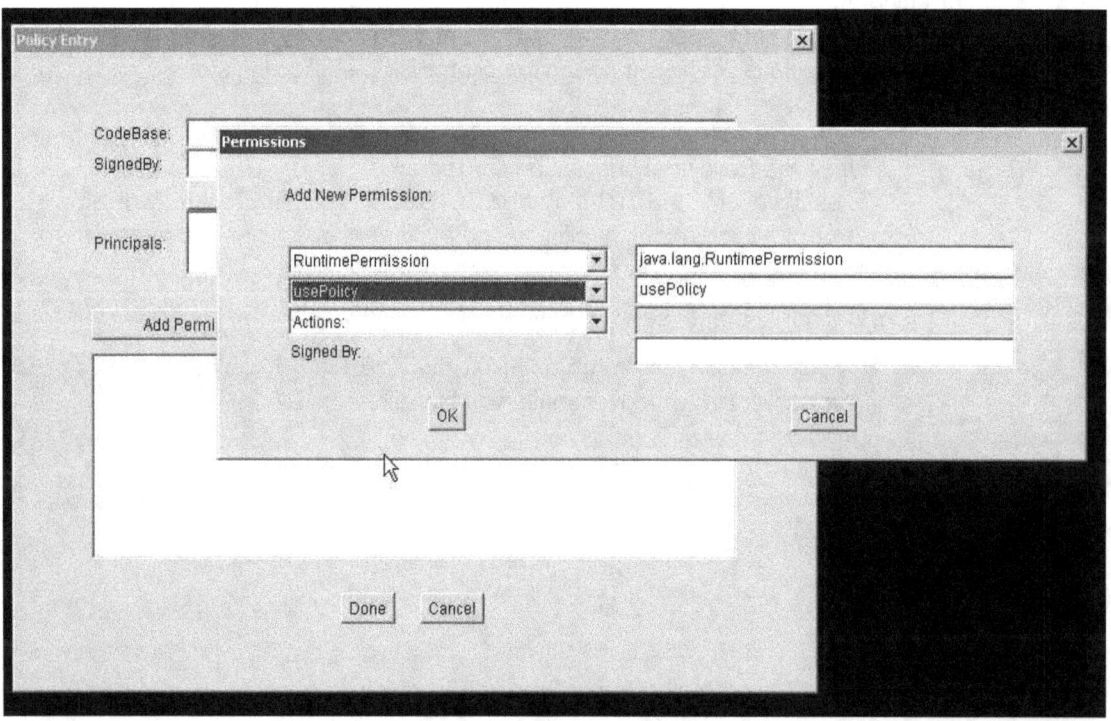

Figure 9 - The usePolicy Policy Entry

- Click Done.

- In the File menu, select Save. (The policy tool will report that it has saved the file.)

- In the File menu, click Exit.

This will generate an entry in the java.policy file that looks like this:

```
grant {
    permission java.lang.RuntimePermission "usePolicy";
};
```

While it is possible to edit the Java.policy file through a text editor, Sun recommends that the Policytool be used.

- ### Adding permissions for specific applets

Adding permissions for specific applets will break signed Java applets that rely on additional permissions. In the ideal case, the developer of these applets will provide a list of permissions specifying the extra permissions actually required by the applet. Not all applets will come with a specific permissions list. Only if the applet is trusted should the administrator consider granting permissions. The tedious process of trial and error works best in figuring out which permissions are required for the applet to run. Only under development or extraordinary circumstances should you completely trust a Java applet developer, only then should the applet be given the AllPermission privilege.

If this applet should be trusted with extra permissions according to your policy, you can give these permissions to specific applets by performing the following steps:

- Open the java.policy file with the Policy Tool.

- Click Add Policy Entry.

- Perform one or both of the following actions to specify which applets this permission entry will apply to:

  - Next to CodeBase, give the full URL to the applet (such as https://www.fakeserver.com/applets/applets.jar). Note that giving a https URL gives an assured channel to the server.

  - Next to SignedBy, give the alias for the public key that was used in the pubcerts keystore. This is how a trusted source can be specified.

- Repeat the following steps for each permission needed.

  - Click Add Permission.

  - Select the specific permission mentioned by the applet developer, or by pulling Permission: down to that permission. (e.g. FilePermission)

    - Select the specific Target Name, if applicable. (e.g. test.txt)

    - Select the specific Actions, if applicable. (e.g. read and write)

  - It is best to only provide vital privileges. If the applet only needs read/ write access on one file, then do not include unnecessary files or commands.

- Click OK.

- Click Done.

- In the File menu, select Save. (The policy tool will report that it has saved the file.)

- In the File menu, click Exit.

This will generate an entry in the java.policy file that looks like this:

```
grant signedBy "Curt",  codeBase "https://www.fakeserver.com/applets/applets.jar"
{
    permission java.io.FilePermission "test.txt", "read, write", signedBy "Curt";
};
```

File Replication for Deployment

For all of these actions to take effect throughout the network, the file java.policy, the file cacerts, and the file pubcerts must be distributed to all machines that use the Java plug-in. This will have to be repeated every time the policy changes (such as if another code-signing certificate is trusted). This can be implemented manually.

Alternatively, this can be performed using a network share. Start by creating a read only network share containing the master java.policy, cacerts, and pubcerts files. Then, overwrite the current java.policy, cacerts and pubcerts for each client. The per-client step could be automated to reduce on maintenance. Whenever the master files are modified for a newly signed applet, then each client will need to be updated.

Known Limitations

JSSE Now Integrated

Java Secure Socket Extension (JSSE) is integrated into the J2SE SDK 1.4. The JSSE API is now installed and utilized by default in the J2SE SDK. This differs greatly from the optional JSSE package in J2SE JDK 1.3 version, which required additional steps of downloading and installing JSSE. The JSSE is now used with the JRE plug-in, forcing any Java applet SSL based communication to use the JRE keystore, cipher settings, and all other certificate-based options instead of the well-maintained browser settings. By enabling JSSE, the administrator is now forced to maintain both the browser certificate settings and the JRE keystore settings.

Lack of the Deny option

Currently, the Java 2 security model does not have a "Deny" option for permissions. A "Deny" option would prove to be useful in many of the permissions, especially the file permission group. For example, if a user has a directory of 100 files and only 3 draft files need to be restricted. The current mechanism is to either grant all 100 files the permission or to individually list the 97 permitted files. However, the "Deny" option would permit the ability to restrict access to the 3 draft files, while still granting access to the 97 other relevant files through the all files choice.

References

"Default Policy Implementation and Policy File Syntax".
http://java.sun.com/j2se/1.4.2/docs/guide/security/PolicyFiles.html , April 2002.

"Java 2 Plug-in 1.4.2 Developer Guide".
http://java.sun.com/j2se/1.4.2/docs/guide/plugin/developer_guide/contents.html

"Java 2 SDK Tools and Utilities".
http://java.sun.com/j2se/1.4.2/docs/tooldocs/tools.html

"Java Secure Socket Extension for the Java 2 SDK, SE, V1.4".
http://java.sun.com/products/jsse/index-14.html

"Java Upgrade Guide: Migrating from the Microsoft VM for Java to the Sun JRE".
http://java.sun.com/j2se/1.4.2/docs/guide/deployment/deployment-guide/upgrade-guide/

"Permissions in the Java 2 SDK".
http://java.sun.com/j2se/1.4.2/docs/guide/security/permissions.html

"Transitioning from the Microsoft Java Virtual Machine".
http://www.microsoft.com/mscorp/java/ , October 2003.

"Using the Java Plug-in Control Panel to Set Plug-in Behavior/Options".
http://java.sun.com/j2se/1.4.2/docs/guide/plugin/developer_guide/control_panel.html

Wrox Press. "Java Security Evolution, Part 2".
http://www_106.ibm.com/developerworks/java/library/j-secevol2/index.html , February 2001.

www.ingramcontent.com/pod-product-compliance
Lightning Source LLC
Chambersburg PA
CBHW080811290526
45790CB00008B/3662